Knowing Your Purpose

Foundational Principles for Discovering and Walking in Your Divine Purpose

Bishop Dr. Frankie H. Young, Th.M., D.D.

H.E.M. Publishing
Detroit, Michigan

Copyright © 2002 Bishop Dr. Frankie H. Young, Th.M., D.D.

ALL RIGHTS RESERVED. *No part of this publication may be translated, reproduced or transmitted in any form or by any means, electronic or mechanical, including photocopy, recording, or any information storage and retrieval system, without permission in writing from the publisher.*

ISBN 0-923568-53-0

H.E.M. Publishing
P.O. BOX 4005
DETROIT, MI 48223

Library of Congress Cataloging-in-Publication Data

Young, Frankie H., 1944-
Knowing your purpose : foundational principles for discovering and
walking in your divine purpose / Frankie H. Young.
p. cm.
ISBN 0-923568-53-0
1. Christian life. 2. Providence and government of God. I. Title.
BV4509.5.Y67 2003
248.4—dc22
2003014770

PRINTED IN THE UNITED STATES OF AMERICA

This book is dedicated to all those who desire to fulfill their purpose in life.

A very special thanks to my husband, Kevin, who encouraged me to write.

I would be remiss without thanking Lytia Rondeau, my scribe, and all those who tirelessly worked to assist me. Thank you.

About the Author

Apostle Dr. Frankie H. Young, BBS, Th.M., DD, is founder and Senior Pastor of Hope Evangelical Ministries.

As Bishop, she presides over the diocese of Hope Evangelical Ministries, a large urban ministry that has affiliations throughout the world. Bishop Young is internationally renown for spiritual insights and clear, concise understanding of the Word of God. This dynamic gift to the body of Christ is a much sought-after speaker and lecturer throughout the world.

As Dr. Young, she is the chancellor of Hope Ecclesiastical Studies International, which has worldwide affiliations.

This visionary has birthed and/or assisted several pastors and noted theologians throughout the world. The wisdom of God that is upon her is evidenced by the excellence with which she demands, first from herself, and then from those who are within her sphere of influence.

Finally, Dr. Frankie H. Young is an author, songwriter and instructor, as well as a wife, mother and grandmother.

Table of Contents

Preface	vi
Introduction	1
Chapter 1 Defining Terms	7
Chapter 2 The Plan of Man for Himself	11
Chapter 3 The Plan of God for Mankind	19
Chapter 4 God Wants to Reveal His Plan to You	35
Chapter 5 You Must Seek God for His Plan Concerning You	53
Chapter 6 Once the Purpose & Plan are Revealed	67
Chapter 7 Knowing Your Purpose	77
Chapter 8 God May Have More for You	81
The Author's Heart	85
Closing Prayer	86

Preface

This book was taken from a taped (audio) series of messages that I delivered to our congregation several years ago.

So many people have no idea that they were created with a definite purpose in mind. God never intended for you to aimlessly go through life without accomplishing His plan for you.

As impossible as it may seem, you were always the hope of God for Him to affect mankind, even this entire earth, with your presence. God has placed within each one of us His creative ability to fulfill His vision on earth.

What a unique person you are, to the extent that God chose you even before the foundations of the world to take part in His ultimate plan for mankind. You were always with God in spirit before you were conceived and brought forth.

It is no mistake that you have such a burning desire to be used by God, yearning to know why you were created. This longing is within you to cause an enthusiastic outcry to God, "What is my purpose?" "Why was I born?"

God's desire for you is to seek Him with your whole heart and soul; and in doing so, God will begin to disclose His desires for you. You can know without any doubt your purpose and how to achieve it.

The purpose of this book is to give you some clarity as to what you must do to understand and fulfill your purpose. If you read this book and apply its principles, it will assist you in your pursuit of God.

Introduction
✦ ✦ ✦

In the process of planning and deciding the purpose for our existence, we generally begin at the goals we would like to accomplish in life. This includes those in the Body of Christ, as well as those who have yet to confess that Jesus Christ is their Lord and Savior. Generally in this method of planning, we base our entire lives around the end result that we expect for our lives and the lives of our offspring, and sometimes we forget about God, the Father Almighty, Creator of all things. Somehow we, even those within the Body of Christ, neglect to ask the Creator why He created us. We overlook the fact that the All Knowing God has a reason for everything that He does, even our existence.

> *"There are many devices in a man's heart; nevertheless the counsel of the LORD, that shall stand." (Proverbs 19:21 KJV)*

> *"O LORD, I know that the way of man is not in himself: it is not in man that walketh to direct his steps." (Jeremiah 10:23 KJV)*

However, God does have a plan for us…each of us…the saved, the unsaved and the refuse-to-be-saved. We all have a role to play in God's absolute plan. There is a purpose that He has intended for each and every one of our lives, from beginning to end.

Can you believe that? Some people have been told that their birth was not planned, or maybe not even wanted. Many carry this stigma all of their lives. Well, here is good news for you. There are no mistakes in God. God Himself gave you forethought and created you, allowed you to be born to reveal His glory. Everything that God made has purpose in the universe, every person, every insect, every tree, fowls of the air, fish of the sea, all have a very definite purpose to fulfill. Just think how chaotic the earth would be if God had not had a definite and distinct plan for all of His creation. How unbalanced the world would be if we all had the same thoughts, visions or even the same tastes. If we all were doctors and there were no nurses, or we all were pastors and there were no parishioners, what an imbalance that would be and how dull and unfruitful. So much would go unexplored and unaccomplished.

> *"In him we were also chosen, having been predestined according to the plan of him who works out everything in conformity with the purpose of his will." (Ephesians 1:11 NIV)*

Introduction

> *"But rise and stand upon thy feet: for I have appeared to thee for this purpose, to make thee a minister and a witness both to these things which thou hast seen, and of those things in the which I will appear to thee." (Acts 26:16 KJV)*

> *"For the scripture saith unto Pharaoh, Even for this same purpose have I raised thee up, that I might shew my power in thee, and that my name might be declared throughout all the earth." (Romans 9:17 KJV)*

Miraculously, God desires to reveal His plan to us. What was once a mystery is now available to all that genuinely desire to know His divine will for their lives.

> *"And he said unto them, Unto you it is given to know the mystery of the kingdom of God: but unto them that are without, all these things are done in parables." (Mark 4:11 KJV)*

> *"Even the mystery which hath been hid from ages and generations, but now is made manifest to his saints." (Colossians 1:26 KJV)*

God wants us to know His will for us so that we can begin to accomplish those tasks that He has assigned to us. He wants us to know that our end result is not in the material things of this world, nor in the inheritance that we leave to our offspring, but in eternal life and salvation (which includes all of the above).

> *"The eyes of your understanding being enlightened; that ye may know what is the hope of His calling, and what the riches of the glory of his inheritance in the saints."*
> *(Ephesians 1:18 KJV)*

Though God wants us to know His plan (our purpose for existing), He won't force His will upon us. He has graciously given us the ability to decide for ourselves. Therefore, we must seek God for His plan and purpose for our lives.

God is love. He wants you to submit your will to Him because you love Him and not from constraint. The human race has been given the ability to think, reason and make choices. The Holy Spirit will not force you to seek Him or submit. This is a choice that you have to make for yourself. Your will is not stronger than God's. Nothing is. God has simply given you the privilege to decide.

> *"If any man lack wisdom, let him ask of God, that giveth to all men liberally, and upbraideth not; and it shall be given him."*
> *(James 1:5 KJV)*

We must hunger after it as we do the things of this world, persistently and consistently performing all that is necessary to obtain His divine blueprint for our lives.

Have you ever desired something so strongly that you were willing to do anything in your power to obtain it? Something as simple as an appetite or craving. You would drive that extra mile or pay the extra cost to appease your craving or hunger, or work the extra overtime to buy that special dress. Well, this is the way that God wants us to seek Him, to hunger for

Introduction

spiritual things, to have knowledge of His thoughts regarding us. Seek God at all costs. As rewarding as wearing that new dress may be or as fulfilling as that hamburger that you drove miles to have may be, even more so will the plan of God for your life be when you fulfill your purpose. Hunger simply means to have a strong, compelling desire or craving.

> **"As the hart panteth after the water brooks, so panteth my soul after thee, O God. My soul thirsteth for God, for the living God: when shall I come and appear before God?" (Psalm 42:1-2KJV)**

The Hebrew word for panteth in this scripture is *"arag"* meaning to long for, cry, pant. Don't you know that when your heart is turned toward God in this way, He will hear and answer your heart's cry. Hallelujah!

> **"Delight thyself also in the LORD; and he shall give thee the desires of thine heart." (Psalm 37:4 KJV)**

Then, once God's plan is revealed to us, we must continue to seek Him for guidance in our daily walk.

> **"Commit thy way unto the LORD; trust also in him; and he shall bring it to pass." (Psalm 37:5 KJV)**

We must be patient and allow God to be God. We must understand His principles and know that they are unchanging. He has always and will always give the increase or bring the plan to fruition.

> *"God is not a man, that he should lie; neither the son of man, that he should repent: hath he said it, and shall he not do it? or hath he spoken, and shall he not make it good?" (Numbers 23:19 KJV)*

Finally, when the appointed time comes, we must walk in our purpose and fulfill the plan that God has already predestined and preordained for our lives. We must walk upright and remember always that it is He who made us; it is He who assigned the task; it is He (in His mercy and grace) who appointed us to do His will in the earth.

> *"I THEREFORE, the prisoner of the Lord, appeal to and beg you to walk (lead a life) worthy of the [divine] calling to which you have been called [with behavior that is credit to the summons to God's service...]" (Ephesians 4:1 AMP)*

We must also remember that though Jesus had an ultimate goal, He had many missions during His journey to the cross. As He fulfilled the plan of the Father in obedience and humility, He was allowed to continue on to fulfill His ultimate goal in the earth. Such may be the same for you. You must know your purpose, walk in your purpose, and continuously seek the guidance of the Father Almighty as you go on to your ultimate place in the Body of Christ Jesus.

Chapter 1

✦ ✦ ✦

Defining Terms

It is important that we have a common understanding of the terminology that will be used throughout this book. We must understand the meaning of these terms as used by the world and as they are used in the biblical context.

Since biblical text has been translated from the Hebrew (Old Testament) and Greek (New Testament) languages, we should understand that the context that a word is being used, even though it is the same word, may have a completely different meaning. Definitions are derived from *The New Webster's Dictionary* and *The New Strong's Complete Dictionary of Bible Words* (in both Hebrew and Greek translations).

Know

> *The New Webster's Dictionary*
> ✧ to apprehend with the conscious mind; to be acquainted with by experience; to have acquired skill in; to realize

The New Strong's Complete Dictionary of Bible Words

- ◆ Hebrew—bîyn (bene) to understand; discern
- ◆ Greek—eidō (i'-do) be aware; behold; consider; perceive; see; tell; understand

Purpose

The New Webster's Dictionary

- ◆ a result which is desired to be obtained; willpower

The New Strong's Complete Dictionary Bible Words

- ◆ Hebrew—'êtsâh (ay-tsaw')—advice; plan; prudence; counsel
- ◆ Greek—prothĕsis (proth'-es'is)—a setting forth; intention

Plan

The New Webster's Dictionary

- ◆ a design for construction; layout; system; a scheme; a proposed course of action

Mission

The New Webster's Dictionary

- ◆ an aim in life; arising from a conviction

Predestinated

The New Webster's Dictionary

- ◆ determined beforehand

Defining Terms

The New Strong's Complete Dictionary of Bible Words

⬥ Greek—proorizō (pro-or-id´-zo)—to limit in advance; to determine before; ordain

Revelation

The New Webster's Dictionary

⬥ to make known; to expose to view

The New Strong's Complete Dictionary of Bible Words

⬥ Greek—apokalupsis (ap-ok-al´-oop-sis)—disclosure; appearing; coming; lighten; manifestation; to take off the cover; be revealed

Wisdom

The New Webster's Dictionary

⬥ intelligence drawing on experience and governed by prudence; a store of knowledge

The New Strong's Complete Dictionary of Bible Words

⬥ Hebrew—sekel (seh´-kel) or sêkel (say´-kel)—intelligence; success; discretion; knowledge; policy; prudence; sense; understanding

⬥ Greek—phronēsis (fron´-ay-sis)—intellectual or moral insight: prudence

Chapter One Reflections

1. Did you study the terms identified in this chapter?

2. Did you commit these words to memory?

3. Can you give meaning to these words in your own terminology?

4. How many more words can you add to this list? Please do so.

Chapter 2

✦ ✦ ✦

The Plan of Man for Himself

What is your purpose in life? What action plan have you entered into in order to fulfill this purpose? Does your plan include God, your Creator? Have you sought God for His plan for you?

There are many people who have entered into the prime of their adult life and are still searching for their purpose for existing. They jump from job to job, school to school, social club to social club, and religious belief to religious belief. They constantly find themselves saying, "I just didn't fit in. It wasn't the right place for me. I'm trying to find my niche. It's time for a change. Something's missing in my life." Oftentimes these are people who have accomplished every goal that they had set for themselves. Those goals, they thought, would bring them happiness, a feeling of contentment and completeness. However, something is still missing.

On the other hand, there are those who think they have their purpose in life all figured out. From childhood it was already decided which schools they would attend, which social groups they would become members of, which churches they would join. They have accomplished everything that they wanted to accomplish in life. They have followed in the path of their parents or the way of their friends. They have the 'perfect' job, the 'perfect' mate, 'perfect' children, and they even attend church some Sundays. Their lives are 'perfect'—picture-perfect—in their eyes. They busy themselves with the things of the world, the ideals of society, and consume themselves with material gain. However, whether they realize it or not, something is still missing.

It is good to have goals in life. Everyone desires to have a good family life, a wonderful mate, and children who are following in their footsteps (only the good steps). It is normal to want to be financially secure; to be able to afford the finer things that this life has to offer. Isn't it a great thing to be politically correct and to belong to the right social group. How much better is it to say that you are religious, share a popular belief, and belong to a well-known church.

There is nothing wrong with having goals in life. Goals provide direction and ultimately keep us focused. However, a plan that does not include God, the Creator of all things, is a plan for failure. Have you ever met anyone that seems to have it all together yet is not fulfilled? That is a person most miserable.

> *"Except the LORD build the house, they labour in vain that build it: except the LORD keep the city, the watchman waketh but in vain." (Psalm 127:1 KJV)*

The Plan of Man For Himself

God wants His people to be prosperous. Your desire to be prosperous is not greater than God's desire for you. Just as your desire for your children is to have tremendous success in life, His will for you is the same. He simply wants you to seek Him as to how to accomplish it, so that He will be glorified.

"...Let the LORD be magnified, which hath pleasure in the prosperity of his servant." (Psalm 35:27 KJV)

God wants His people to have good marriages and obedient children. How important is it for you to have a good marriage and children that are supportive, assisting you and your plan for life? I believe that it is one of Satan's strategies to have you marry the wrong person so that you abort the will of God for your life. For there to be harmony in the home, there must first be agreement. Where there is no agreement, there will be conflict, diverting your attention and efforts from God's plan for you. You and your family will suffer as a result. If you are single, be very prayerful in selecting a mate. Your destiny depends upon it. Many people have suffered and some yet suffer because of being unequally yoked, causing them years of pain, delay or unfulfilled desires. If you are married and find yourself in this dilemma, pray for your mate, asking God to heal your marriage so that the two of you may become one. God is faithful.

"Blessed is every one that feareth the LORD; that walketh in his ways. For thou shalt eat the labour of thine hands; happy shalt thou be, and it shall be well with thee. Thy wife shall be as a fruitful vine by the sides of thine

house: thy children like olive plants round about thy table. Behold, that thus shall the man be blessed that feareth the LORD." (Psalm 128: 1-4 KJV)

God encourages us to pursue higher learning. Education is very important and may be crucial to your destiny, both spiritual and secular. We live in a very technologically high ("high-tech") society. You must be trained to the very best of your ability to fulfill your calling. The day is spent where you only need the anointing. Thank God for the anointing, but you need skill also. You must perfect the gift that God has given. As the gift is perfected in you, an even greater anointing will flow. God loves excellence.

"And he that sent me is with me: the Father hath not left me alone; for I do always those things that please him." (John 8:29 KJV)

"Study to show thyself approved unto God, a workman that needeth not to be ashamed, rightly dividing the word of truth." (II Timothy 2:15 KJV)

God even wants us to commune with the right group of people. Connecting with the right people is very important. Who are your friends? Who are you allowing to speak into your life? Do they believe in you? What accomplishments have they made in their lives that can benefit you? Are they supportive, optimistic or pessimistic? If they are not helping, they are hindering. This may sound harsh to some, but remember what Jesus said about the unprofitable branches. Good has invested Himself in you to receive a profit. Sur-

The Plan of Man For Himself

round yourself with positive people that can make a deposit into your life.

> *"Every branch in me that beareth not fruit he taketh away: and every branch that beareth fruit, he purgeth it, that it may bring forth more fruit." (John 15:2 KJV)*

> *"And now also the axe is laid unto the root of the trees: therefore every tree which bringeth not forth good fruit is hewn down, and cast into the fire." (Matthew 3:10 KJV)*

Remember, God expects us to bring forth "good" fruit, that which He Himself has placed within us in the form of seed. That seed is His vision.

> *"For by wise counsel thou shalt make thy war: and in multitude of counselors there is safety." (Proverbs 24:6 KJV)*

> *"Where no counsel is, the people fall: but in the multitude of counselors there is safety." (Proverbs 11:14 KJV)*

> *"Without counsel purposes are disappointed: but in the multitude of counselors they are established." (Proverbs 15:22 KJV)*

Yet, in all the things that He wants for us, we must remember that our way of thinking differs greatly from His.

> *"For as the heavens are higher than the earth, so are my ways higher than your ways,*

and my thoughts than your thoughts."
(Isaiah 55:9 KJV)

Most people, whether they are a part of the Body of Christ or not, will agree that there is a higher being...an almighty and all powerful being that created all things. Better yet, most will even agree that there is a purpose for which they were born. Ironically, if those same individuals were asked if they sought this higher power, this almighty being (who those in the Body of Christ know as the Almighty God, Creator of all things) for their ultimate purpose for existing, most would answer, "No."

Oddly enough, there are those within the Body of Christ that sit in church service after service, yet they have not thought to ask the God that they worship what His plan is for them. It is imperative that we in the Body of Christ know the purpose that God has for our lives. It is easy to plan career and educational goals and even easier to work in a chosen field. However, it is fruitless in the eyes of God if our personal goal is to become the President of the United States when God has called us to be a full-time minister, and we neglect to pursue His call. Even greater, it is reckless to lock ourselves into becoming a local church pastor when God has called us to be an international evangelist, thereby dimming the light that He has already predestined to shine.

Moreover, it is important that those in positions of leadership in the Body of Christ continuously seek God for the daily planning of their lives. It is not enough to know that God has called you into a position of leadership in your ministry. It is not enough to attend every church service, sing in the choir and tithe your tithes. You must diligently seek God

The Plan of Man For Himself

daily because His daily plan for you may change based upon His ultimate purpose for your life. God may have called you to be a Sunday school teacher last year, but this year, because of your faithful service, God has chosen to move you on to the next phase of His plan by appointing you an Elder in your ministry. Yet, if you neglect to seek His plan for you each and every day, the end result may be walking outside of His will. God is ever moving; therefore, becoming complacent or stagnant may cause Him to move to another to bring His plan into fruition. Don't be afraid to change with the flow of the anointing. Don't become so locked in on what you presently enjoy doing that you can't accept change.

We must remember always that God is a God of plan and purpose. He is a God of timing and order. Finally, God is a God of fulfillment and completion, and the purpose that God had for you, when He allowed you to become manifested in your mother's womb, will be accomplished. You may change your mind about pursuing God's plan, however, He never does. He will get you back on track. God has confidence in you even when you don't have confidence in yourself.

> *"To every thing there is a season, and a time to every purpose under the heaven." (Ecclesiastes 3:1 KJV)*

> *"Before I formed thee in the belly I knew thee; and before thou camest forth out of the womb I sanctified thee, and I ordained thee a prophet unto the nations." (Jeremiah 1:5 KJV)*

Chapter Two Reflections

1. Do you know your purpose?

2. Whose plan are you following, yours or God's?

3. Are you fulfilled with your accomplishments? If yes, how do you know?

4. What natural goals do you have?

5. What spiritual goals do you have?

6. How do you measure prosperity?

7. Are you associating with people that believe in your purpose (future)?

8. Are your thoughts the same as God's thoughts? How do you know?

9. Do you seek God daily for direction?

Keep a journal of His direction leading to your purpose.

Chapter 3

✦ ✦ ✦

The Plan of God for Mankind

The Reason God Created Man

The reason that God created man was so that He could be glorified in the earth.

"Thy people also shall be all righteous: They shall inherit the land for ever, the branch of my planting, the work of my hands, that I may be glorified." (Isaiah 60:21 KJV)

In the beginning, Lucifer was thrown out of the Kingdom of God and fell onto the face of the earth, causing utter havoc and confusion.

> *"How art thou fallen from heaven, O Lucifer, son of the morning! How art thou cut down to the ground, which did weaken the nations! For thou hast said in thine heart, I will ascend into heaven, I will exalt my throne above the stars of God: I will sit also upon the mount of the congregation, in the sides on the north:" (Isaiah 12-13 KJV)*

Lucifer (now Satan), who only wanted to be worshipped and glorified, inhabited the earth alone with the rest of the fallen angels that rebelled with him in heaven. After God reinforced His power and victory over Satan by restoring the earth back to the form in which He originally created it, He created man to rule and have dominion in the earth. Otherwise, Satan would have been in possession of the earth alone and the other fallen angels would have worshipped him as God.

> *"I will ascend above the heights of the clouds: I will be like the most High." (Isaiah 14:14 KJV)*

Therefore, man was created to glorify God by constantly reinforcing Satan's defeat.

> *"Through thee will we push down our enemies, through thy name will we tread them under that rise up against us." (Psalm 44:5 KJV)*

> *"Behold, I give unto you power to tread on serpents and scorpions, and over all the power of the enemy: and nothing shall by any means harm you." (St. Luke 10:19 KJV)*

Man was created to reign as a god in the earth, subject to only God the Father.

> *"What is man, that thou art mindful of him? And the son of man, that thou visitest him? For thou hast made him a little lower than the angels [Elohim], and hast crowned him with glory and honour. Thou madest him to have dominion over the works of thine hands; thou has put all things under his feet:" (Psalm 8:4-6 KJV)*

> *"I have said, Ye are gods; and all of you are children of the most High." (Psalm 82:6 KJV)*

> *"Jesus answered and said unto them, Is it not written in your law, I said, Ye are gods? If he called them gods, unto whom the word of God came, and the scripture cannot be broken." (St. John 10:34-35 KJV)*

However, because of the sin or transgression of Adam in the Garden of Eden, sin and rebellion entered into the world, making an obvious defeat a constant battle. Therefore, man had to be redeemed back into the presence of God before he could take his rightful place of authority over Satan. Thus the battle began.

> *"And I will put enmity between thee and the woman, and between thy seed and her seed; it shall bruise thy head, and thou shalt bruise his heel." (Genesis 3:15 KJV)*

Whereas God's original instruction to man was to have dominion over the land and multiply (be fruitful), His earnest goal is to redeem man back into the Kingdom of God before Satan causes his demise.

Illustration of God's Plan for Man in Jesus Christ

Before the female Adam contemplated eating the forbidden fruit, God had already instituted the plan for Jesus the Christ.

> *"They are the ones whose names were not written in the Book of Life, which belongs to the Lamb who was killed before the world was made." (Revelation 13:8 NLT)*

The Word of God says that He knows all of our thoughts; therefore, He knew the sin of Adam even before Adam committed it.

> *"For I know their works and their thoughts..." (Isaiah 66:18 KJV)*

Keeping in mind the reason that God created man—to be glorified by having dominion (rule) in the earth—the All Knowing, Almighty God had no intention of forfeiting His already pronounced victory because of the sin of one man. As such, the plan of Jesus began. Throughout the Word of God from the time Adam and now Eve (prior to the fall of man both were called Adam by God—Genesis 2:23; 3:20) were thrown out of the Garden of Eden, God systematically sent people into the earth to lay the foundation for the coming of the Messiah (the consecrated one) who would come to redeem man back into the presence of God.

> ***"And I will put enmity between thee and the woman, and between thy seed and her seed; it shall bruise thy head, and thou shalt bruise his heel." (Genesis 3:15 KJV)***

> ***"For it is not possible that the blood of bulls and of goats should take away sins. Wherefore, when he [Jesus] cometh into the world, he saith, Sacrifice and offering thou wouldest not, but a body hast thou prepared me: In burnt offerings and sacrifices for sin thou hast no pleasure. Then said I [Jesus], Lo I come to do thy will. Then said he, Lo, I came to do thy will, O God. He taketh away the first that He may establish the second." (Hebrews 10: 4-7, 9 KJV)***

God in His infinite wisdom even gave instruction, signs, examples, words, and visions to the people, now nations, through His chosen vessels to help them to recognize their salvation when He arrived. God knew even still that of those He brought into the earth, they would still reject this Salvation for various reasons. Yet in His mercy and grace, He added miracles and mighty works to be wrought through this individual (Jesus) to prove a more compelling fact; that He was indeed the Chosen One.

> *"If I do not the works of my Father, believe me not. But if I do, though ye believe not me, believe the works: that ye may know, and believe that the Father is in me, and I in him." (St. John 10:37-38 KJV)*

In the same manner did God orchestrate your birth for his ultimate plan and purpose in the earth. As such, it is important that we know the purpose for our existence so that we can begin to walk in the plan for which we were created.

God's Plan for Man Differs from Man's Plan for Himself

God's plan for man often differs from the plan of man for himself. Even Christ Jesus, when facing the final step of faith toward the cross said:

> *"...Father, if thou be willing, remove this cup from me: nevertheless not my will, but thine, be done." (Luke 22:42 KJV)*

Thus indicating, that had Jesus been given any input in the final stages of His walk on earth, there was something He may have done differently. However, in His obedience, He drank from the cup that He requested be taken away. This was God...the God that walked the earth. Yes, if given the opportunity, He may have done something a little differently, yet He conceded that the will of God was far greater and much more rewarding than His own.

Such is the same for us. Oftentimes, there are things that we desire to do and places that we desire to go that are not in the will of God for our lives. There are even places that we know for a fact that God has called us to that we run wholeheartedly away from because the sacrifice is too great. If you are going to fulfill the perfect will of God for your life, you must be willing to die to your own agenda, thoughts and beliefs. Your success in God is predicated upon your total obedience. Oftentimes, in fact most of the time, you will not understand what God is requiring of you. However, as you continue to seek God and His will, you will experience that it all truly worked for your good.

Like Jesus, we know our end (if we are obedient) is everlasting life and eternal glory.

> *"But he that shall endure unto the end, the same shall be saved." (Matthew 24:13 KJV)*

> *"And ye shall be hated of all men for my name's sake: but he that shall endure unto the end, the same shall be saved." (Mark 13:13 KJV)*

> *"Blessed is the man that endureth temptation: for when he is tried, he shall receive the crown of life, which the Lord hath promised to them that love him." (James 1:12 KJV)*

However, the circumstances of our walk can sometimes be so overwhelming that we lose sight of the promised end, and make the plea of Jesus... "if thou will let this cup be taken from me..." Somehow, we forget the latter part of Jesus' plea, "...nevertheless, not my will but thy will be done." Many of us forget to submit to the will of God; to stand in the face of the troubling adversity and complete the mission to the end. We often pray and ask God to reveal His plan, purpose and will to us, however, we are not willing and ready to accept the method of God. We must remember that it is just as important for us to submit to God's ordained method for fulfilling our purpose, as it is for us to complete the purpose.

We are not the first, nor the last to be guilty of this character flaw. The Word of God details numerous examples of those who knew their purpose (or a portion thereof), yet they did not totally submit to the method of God. Those who were initially out of the will of God, yet by submitting to the method they fulfilled their purpose. And finally, the One who knew the plan, submitted to the method and totally fulfilled the purpose for which He was intended (that person being Christ Jesus).

Now Abraham received instruction from God coupled with a promise.

> ***"Get thee out of thy country, and away from thy father's house, unto a land that I will show thee: and I will make of thee a great nation, and I will bless thee, and make thy name great; and thou shalt be a blessing." (Genesis 12:1-2 KJV)***

Abraham received the Word of God and obeyed the instruction of God, with one minor exception.

> **"And Abram [Abraham] departed, as the LORD had spoken unto him; and Lot went with him..." (Genesis 12:4 KJV)**

How awesome. Abraham received the Word of the Lord and stepped out on faith! He left all that he knew in obedience to God's Word. Not so. Yes, Abraham received the Word of the Lord. Yes, Abraham left the only home that he'd ever known. Yes, this was an extreme leap of faith. However, he did not submit to the total method of God. He allowed Lot to accompany him. This tiny variance later caused Abraham much frustration, grief and loss of a portion of substance that God had given him.

> **"And Abraham said unto Lot, Let there be no strife, I pray thee between me and thee, and between my herdmen and thy herdmen; for we be brethren. Is not the whole land before thee? Separate thyself, I pray thee, from me: if thou wilt take the left hand, then I will go to the right; or if thou depart to the right hand, then I will go to the left." (Genesis 13:8-9 KJV)**

However, God sincerely desires to fulfill all of His promises to each of us, even when we take 'minor' detours to His divine instruction. For as soon as Abraham was separated from Lot, the Lord immediately restored all that he'd surrendered to Lot and much, much more! Now, isn't that the love of God; even when we make all types of blunders, God is there, waiting and faithfully getting us back on course.

> *"And the Lord said to Abram, after that Lot was separated from him, Lift up now thine eyes, and look from the place where thou art northward, and southward, and eastward, and westward: For all that thou seest, to thee will I give it, and to thy seed for ever." (Genesis 13:14-15 KJV)*

Moses, for instance, received direct and detailed instructions as to a portion of his purpose.

> *"Come now therefore, and I will send thee unto Pharaoh, that thou mayest bring forth my people the children of Israel out of Egypt." (Exodus 3:10 KJV)*

However, his initial response was not, "Lord, thank You so much for choosing me. Since You've revealed my purpose, I know that I can accomplish this awesome task. Be glorified!" On the contrary, Moses actually responded...

> *"Who am I, that I should go unto Pharaoh, and that I should bring forth the children of Israel out of Egypt?" (Exodus 3:11 KJV)*

Moses was not too excited about the method. Yet, he submitted and ultimately completed the mission that God had set before him with great success. Through this mission he became familiar with the voice of God, the ability of God, and the strategic mind of God. He also learned the importance of receiving instruction from God and precisely adhering to it. As a result, Moses had very intimate experiences with God and was considered a friend of God.

We too may come to a place in God where we have gained sensitivity to the voice of God, witnessed the mighty hand of God, experienced an indescribable closeness with God, and have been historically obedient to the instruction of God...to the letter. Yet, we must be constantly aware that history does not necessarily repeat itself, and a single act of disobedience may cause us to disqualify ourselves from receiving the total blessing. Moses is our example of this fate. God gave Moses instruction.

> *"And the Lord spake unto Moses, saying, Take the rod, and gather thou the assembly together, thou, and Aaron thy brother, and speak ye unto the rock before their eyes; and it shall give forth his water, and thou shalt bring forth to them water out of the rock: so thou shalt give the congregation and their beasts drink." (Numbers 20:8 KJV)*

Moses, in anger and frustration with the rebellious people he governed, did not precisely follow the instruction of God.

> *"And Moses took the rod from before the Lord, as he commanded him. And Moses gathered the congregation together before the rock...And Moses lifted up his hand, and with his rod he smote the rock twice..." (Numbers 20: 9-11 KJV)*

As a result of this infringement, Moses was not allowed to lead the people that he'd labored with for many years into the land of promise.

> *"And the Lord spake unto Moses and Aaron, Because ye believed me not, to sanctify me in the eyes of the children of Israel, therefore ye shall not bring this congregation into the land which I have given them." (Numbers 20:12 KJV)*

It is very important that we learn from this tragic mistake of Moses. Sometimes God will give an instruction for you to do something that you have done previously but will change the method. Why is this? Could it be that God does not want us to take anything for granted? He does not want us to assume anything or even begin to think that we have a handle on everything. God's desire is for us to be always sensitive to hear His voice, to receive and obey His instructions to the letter.

I remember my experience in a similar incident. God had given me a word of knowledge to speak to an individual, and in my attempt to make the words smoother, I changed a word that the Holy Spirit had given me to speak. In God's displeasure, I was rebuked sharply. The Holy Spirit spoke, "How dare you attempt to alter what I say? You must always hear and obey exactly what I say." From that moment, I repented and vowed to always obey God. Hallelujah!

Moses did not have the opportunity to correct his act of disobedience, as did Abraham. This one act caused Moses to forfeit a promise of God in his life. We must use Moses' unfortunate example as a catalyst of correction in our lives and a reminder that we must continue in obedience to the Word of God until we have finished our course.

Alternatively, we have the example of the Apostle Paul, who began his journey blinded by deception and working contrary to the will of God. Paul, then Saul, was an opponent to the cause of Jesus Christ, intensely persecuting the church. Saul, like many of us in our former bondages of sin, thought that he was doing what was right. While in sin, you are often under the misconception that you are doing what is right. Attempts to justify the wrong that you have taken part in is common because your eyes are blind. The god of this world (Satan) blinds your eyes or distorts your perception in such a way that you can neither see nor hear truth. At that point, only Jesus can open up your eyes so that you are able to see, hear and comprehend truth.

Such is illustrated in the conversion of the Apostle Paul; one encounter with Jesus transformed him from a feared foe to a formidable champion to the cause of Jesus Christ.

> *"And Saul, yet breathing out threatenings and slaughter against the disciples of the Lord, went unto the high priest, and desired of them letters to Damascus to the synagogues, that if he found any of this way, whether they were men or women, he might bring them bound unto Jerusalem. As he journeyed, he came near Damascus: and suddenly there shined round about him a light from heaven: And he fell to the earth, and heard a voice saying unto him, Saul, Saul, why persecutest thou me? And he said, Who are thou Lord? And the Lord said, I am Jesus whom thou persecutest..." (Acts 9: 1-5 KJV)*

> *"And I [Saul] said, What shall I do, Lord? And he said unto me, Arise and go to Damascus; and there it shall be told thee of all things which are appointed for thee to do."*
> *(Acts 22:10 KJV)*

Paul in turn completed many missionary journeys, spreading the gospel of Christ Jesus. Because of his fervor for the cause of Christ, many souls were won to the Kingdom of God, many churches were planted, many saints were encouraged in their afflictions, much godly wisdom and instruction was given to churches of that time, this time and shall be given in times to come, through the epistles he adorned with much love. Ultimately, Paul had the testimony that all believers should covet; he had finished his course.

What does it mean to finish? The *New Strong's Complete Dictionary of Bible Words* defines finished in the Greek as "teleo," which means to complete, execute, conclude, discharge, accomplish, make an end, expire, fill up, finish, go over, pay or perform. The apostle wrote that the race is not given to the swift, but to the one that endures or finishes purpose. God has given you the grace (His ability) to complete all that He has set before you to accomplish. All right. So you may have made mistakes, you may have missed the mark on occasions. Nevertheless, get up, repent, seek God for instruction and get back in the race. God has planned no defeat for you. Develop a winning attitude and say, "I can do all things through Christ Jesus that dwells in me. Look out world, I am an overcomer! I always win! I am a son of God!"

> *"For I am now ready to be offered up…I have fought a good fight, I have finished my course, I have kept the faith: Henceforth there is laid up for me a crown of righteousness, which the Lord, shall give me at that day…" (II Timothy 4:6-8 KJV)*

Just as Jesus revealed himself to Paul for a purpose, in the same manner He reveals himself to us. Once Jesus has revealed himself, we must, like the Apostle Paul, inquire of the Lord the purpose for His divine revelation. We must ask the Lord why He saved us. His reason is much deeper than saving us from eternal damnation. Even still, after our initial purpose has been revealed, we must ask the Lord for the method. We must say, "Lord, what do you want me to do now?" and remain open to receive further instruction.

Chapter Three Reflections

1. What was Lucifer's first mistake?

2. Way was man created?

3. How did rebellion enter into the world and mankind?

4. What was Adam's (the male) sin?

5. What was God's original instruction to Adam?

6. How and why was Adam, the female's, name changed to Eve?

7. Why do you suppose that God does not allow men (mankind) to determine their own purpose?

8. What was Jesus' reasoning regarding the cup being "removed" from Him?

9. Have you ever prayed that prayer? What was God's response? Did you overcome? How?

10. What was the end result of your obedience/disobedience?

11. In what ways can Jesus reveal Himself to you, helping you to identify your purpose?

12. What can you learn and how can you profit from Moses' mistakes?

Chapter 4

✦ ✦ ✦

God Wants to Reveal His Plan to You

God is a fair and just God. The All-knowing God is fully aware of our daily challenges; whether internal or external, He desires that we be totally equipped to overcome them. God not only has the plan for our lives but the blueprint for every strategy erected against us that would hinder our completion of His plan for our lives.

> *"Behold, I have created the smith that bloweth the coals in the fire, and that bringeth forth an instrument for his work; and I have created the waster to destroy. No weapon that is formed against thee shall prosper..." (Isaiah 54:16-17 KJV)*

This decree of God can only be truly effective in our lives if we know our purpose, have the plan of God and walk in His will.

The Word of God states that weapons will be formed against us. The college dictionary defines a weapon as any instrument or device used for attack or defense in a fight or in combat; anything used against an opponent, adversary or victim. These weapons will not and cannot prosper against you. When you decide to do the will of God for your life, attacks will come to discourage you, to paralyze you, to attempt to make your faith weak. If you are going to pursue God to the end, you will engage in spiritual warfare. You have been given authority to tread upon serpents, not have serpents tread upon you.

> ***"Behold, I give unto you power to tread on serpents and scorpions, and over all the power of the enemy: and nothing shall by any means hurt you." (Luke 10:19 KJV)***

God's Plan for the Prophets of Old

God's track record shows that He has revealed His plan to His servants. God is not respective of persons. Just as He revealed His plan for Adam to Adam; Jeremiah to Jeremiah; Ezekiel to Ezekiel; Mary, the mother of our Lord, to Mary; and His plan for Jesus unto Jesus; so does He desire to reveal His plan to us. Under further examination of the lives of these people, it is also evident and detailed in the Word of God that He only entrusts His plan to those that are willing and ready to be made able to complete the associated tasks. Finally, His plan is restricted from the slothful, hidden from the sensually intellectual, and a stumbling block to His foes. God has reserved His plan for the earnest, sincere, diligent seekers of it; those who also desire whole-heartedly to do His will.

God revealed His plan for Adam immediately after he was created.

> *"So God created man in his own image, in the image of God created he him; male and female created he them. And God said unto them, be fruitful, and multiply, and replenish the earth, and subdue it..." (Genesis 1:27-28 KJV)*

You may be new to the Body of Christ, a baby saint, and feel that it's too soon to know your purpose, to inquire of God's plan for your life. You may feel as if you want to set your own pace. Maybe the accountability of knowing God's will for you is a little more than you care to bear at this juncture of your life. However, the Word of God instructs us to receive God wholly and immediately; this includes knowing His plan.

> *"And straightway he preached Christ in the synagogues, that he is the Son of God." (Acts 9:20 KJV)*

> *"And straightway they forsook their nets, and followed him." (Mark 1:18 KJV)*

Though you are to seek the plan of God for your life, you must be patient and allow God to prepare you for your journey. The Word of God tells us that we must desire the sincere milk of the Word that we may **grow**. Grow simply means to increase in size by a natural (spiritual) process of development, to be enlarged.

> *"As newborn babes, desire the sincere milk of the word, that ye may grow thereby." (I Peter 2:2 KJV)*

The 'ascension' gifts (the five-fold ministry gifts) have been given to the Body of Christ by Jesus Christ so that you can be perfected, nourished and prepared to do the work of the ministry.

> *"And he gave some, apostles; and some, prophets; and some, evangelists; and some, pastors and teachers; For the perfecting of the saints, for the work of the ministry, for the edifying of the body of Christ: Till we all come in the unity of the faith, and of the knowledge of the Son of God, unto a perfect man, unto the measure of the stature of the fullness of Christ: That we henceforth be no more children, tossed to and fro, and carried about with every wind of doctrine, by the sleight of men, and cunning craftiness, whereby they lie in wait to deceive; But speaking the truth in love, may grow up into him in all things, which is the head, even Christ." (Ephesians 4:11-15 KJV)*

The time of leisure and indecision is not afforded to you once you have received Jesus Christ, for He appeared to you for a purpose. He had a plan for you when He removed the scales of deception from your eyes and the cotton of lies from

God Wants to Reveal His Plan To You

your ears. He had a purpose for you when He stopped you on your road to Damascus (your road to destruction). He had a plan for you when he compelled you to repent and be baptized. As such, you need to begin to inquire of God immediately for the purpose that he has for you.

The purpose of God for Jeremiah, the prophet, was revealed to him very clearly and specifically.

> ***"Then the Word of the Lord came unto me, saying, Before I formed thee in the belly I knew thee; and before thou camest forth out of the womb I sanctified thee, and I ordained thee a prophet unto the nations." (Jeremiah 1:5 KJV)***

God not only revealed to Jeremiah his purpose, but when he was chosen, why he was chosen and whom he would affect. Since God has already established this precedence, and we know that He is not a respecter of persons, then we should feel confident that God will reveal our plan to us. Although everyone is not called into the five-fold ministry, we have all been called into the Body of Christ and we all have a purpose for existing that must be fulfilled.

> ***"And he [Jesus] gave some, apostles; and some, prophets; and some evangelists; and some, pastors and teachers." (Ephesians 4:11 KJV)***

> ***"And all things are of God, who hath reconciled us to himself by Jesus Christ, and hath given to us the ministry of reconciliation." (II Corinthians 5:18 KJV)***

The purpose and plan of God for your life may not be glamorous or comfortable. God may call you into a "last-chance-ministry," such as that of the prophet Ezekiel.

> *"And he said unto me [Ezekiel], Son of Man, I send thee to the children of Israel, to a rebellious nation that hath rebelled against me: they and their fathers have transgressed against me, even unto this very day. For they are impudent children and stiffhearted. I do send thee unto them; and thou shalt say unto them, Thus saith the Lord God. And they, whether they will forbear, (for they are a rebellious house,) yet shall know that there hath been a prophet among them." (Ezekiel 2:3-5 KJV)*

Whatever the case, if you truly desire to be effective for God, you must make a quality decision that His purpose and plan for your life is grand, whatever that plan and purpose may be.

God's Plan for Jesus Christ

Before the world was formed Jesus knew His purpose for coming into the earth. He knew His ultimate purpose, which was to destroy the works of the devil.

> *"For this purpose the Son of God was manifested, that he might destroy the works of the devil." (I John 3:8 KJV)*

However, in journeying toward the fulfillment of His ultimate purpose, Jesus was assigned many tasks. Jesus knew all the reasons why He came. He knew all the purposes for which He had been manifested in the earth. He declared them through the prophets of old and personally during His time in the earth.

Jesus knew that he'd come to fulfill the law (the Old Testament prophecies).

> *"Think not that I am come to destroy the law, or the prophets: I am not come to destroy, but to fulfil." (Matthew 5:17 KJV)*

Jesus was aware that He was sent to minister unto and give His life for man.

> *"Even as the Son of Man came not to be ministered unto, but to minister, and to give his life a ransom for many." (Matthew 20:28 KJV)*

Jesus confirmed that He had come to preach, heal, deliver, give sight and liberty to man.

> *"The Spirit of the Lord is upon me, because he hath anointed me to preach the gospel to the poor, he hath sent me to heal the brokenhearted, to preach deliverance to the captives, and recovering of sight to the blind, to set at liberty them that are bruised, to preach the acceptable year of the Lord." (Luke 4:18-19 KJV)*

Jesus clearly proclaimed that He came to save sinners.

> *"...I came not to call the righteous, but sinners to repentance." (Mark 2:17 KJV)*

Jesus came to make manifest sons of God.

> *"Verily, verily, I say unto you, He that believeth on me, the works that I do shall he do also; and greater works than these shall he do; because I go unto my Father." (John 14:12 KJV)*

> *"For as many as are led by the Spirit of God, they are the sons of God. For ye have not received the spirit of bondage again to fear; but ye have received the Spirit of adoption, whereby we cry, Abba, Father. The Spirit itself beareth witness with our spirit, that we are the children of God." (Romans 8:14-16 KJV)*

> *"Behold, what manner of love the Father hath bestowed upon us, that we should be called the sons of God: therefore the world knoweth us not, because it knew him not." (1 John 3:1 KJV)*

Jesus knew that He was only in the earth for an appointed time. He knew that by completing the plan of God, The Father, for His life; He would be highly exalted and seated at the right hand of The Father. Yes, Jesus knew of the glory that awaited Him, but He also knew of the suffering that He needed to endure before He could receive that promise.

Jesus knew that in accomplishing the will of God for His life, there were baptisms that He needed to submit to. In fact, Jesus knew that there were three baptisms that He had to endure. The first was the water baptism.

> *"Then cometh Jesus from Galilee to Jordan unto John, to be baptized of him. But John forbad him, saying, I have need to be baptized of thee, and comest thou to me? And Jesus answering said unto him, Suffer it to be so now: for thus it becometh us to fulfil all righteousness. Then he suffered him."* (Matthew 3:13-15 KJV)

This sacrament is often administered to men with much joy upon their receiving conversion from the ways of the world into the kingdom of God. We submit to this sacrament to identify with the death, burial and resurrection of Christ. This is one of the primary steps to fulfilling the purpose that God has for our lives.

Even Jesus needed the baptism of the Holy Spirit.

> *"And my servant, whom I have chosen; my beloved, in whom my soul is well pleased: I will put my Spirit upon him, and he shall show judgment to the Gentiles."* (Matthew 12:18 KJV)

As He began His earthly ministry unto man, the anointing and the presence of the Holy Spirit was necessary. For Jesus Himself stated that the Spirit of the Lord anointed and sent Him to complete all of the works that He performed as He journeyed to His ultimate purpose.

> *"The Spirit of the Lord is upon me, because he hath anointed me to preach the gospel to the poor; he hath sent me to heal the brokenhearted, to preach deliverance to the cap-*

> *tives, and the recovering of sight to the blind, to set at liberty them that are bruised, To preach the acceptable year of the Lord." (Luke 4:18-19 KJV)*

> *"But if I cast out devils by the Spirit of God, then the Kingdom of God is upon you." (Matthew 12:28 KJV)*

Jesus, who was God manifested in the flesh, submitted to the guidance of the Holy Spirit.

> *"And Jesus being full of the Holy Ghost returned from Jordan, and was led by the Spirit into the wilderness, Being tempted of the devil." (Luke 4: 1-2 KJV)*

Just as it was necessary for Jesus to submit to the leading of the Holy Spirit, we are to submit likewise, even to that of the testing (or trying) of our faith. This is yet another sacrament that most have welcomed or accepted to some extent. We desire to be full of the Holy Spirit, to endure (with success) the trying of our faith, to have the Gifts of the Spirit in operation so that we can do the "greater works" that Jesus Christ decreed that we should perform.

However, there was yet another baptism, a final baptism that Jesus needed to endure before He could be seated; before He could totally accomplish the will of The Father. This baptism is the baptism of Fire.

> *"I indeed baptize you with water unto repentance; but he that cometh after me is mightier than I...He shall baptize you with*

> *the Holy Ghost and with fire." (Matthew 3:11 KJV)*

> *"I am come to send fire on the earth; and what will I, if it be already kindled? But I have a baptism to be baptized with; and how am I straitened till it be accomplished!" (Luke 12:49-50 KJV)*

This is the stage that most don't want to submit to. We don't want to endure this baptism. However, this is a part of the purpose. It's a part of the preparation. It's a part of the exalting. Before you can be exalted, before you can fulfill your total purpose, you must be broken, you must yield, you must repent, and you must endure.

> *"For unto whomsoever much is given, of him shall much be required." (Luke 12:48 KJV)*

> *"The LORD is nigh unto them that are of a broken heart; and saveth such as be of a contrite spirit." (Psalms 34:18 KJV)*

In order for you to totally submit to God, to follow precisely the plan of God; your flesh (your own will) must be consumed by the Fire of the Spirit of God.

> *"In the days of his flesh, Jesus offered up prayers and supplications, with loud cries and tears… Although he was a Son, he learned obedience through what he suffered." (Hebrews 5:7-8 RSV)*

We desire to be disciples of Christ and have accepted the label of "Christian," which means to be Christ-like. We yearn to have the mind of Christ and be transformed into the image and likeness of Christ, yet we don't want to be acquainted with His sufferings. We want to partake of the victory that Jesus wrought for us in the resurrection, yet, as Jesus said to the disciples:

> ***"Are ye able to drink of the cup that I shall drink of and be baptized with the baptism that I am baptized with?" (Matthew 20:22 KJV)***

In seeking the purpose for our lives, we must come to the understanding that God is equitable and just in all of His ways, and His decrees are sure. The Word of God declares that "No flesh shall glory in His presence" (I Corinthians 1:29 KJV). For this reason, the Baptism of Fire comes to destroy the flesh (the carnal man) that would keep us from wholly completing the will of God and entering into His presence.

After such a statement, I must be very careful to explain further. There are those that believe that the abundant life involves no suffering; this is very true. We are not suffering through disease, poverty and torment, we have been set free from all these; but this suffering involves the surrender of your will, the denying of your flesh to sensual pleasures that kill your soul. We suffer because of the dying of the flesh, your own human emotions and practices.

> ***"For I know that in me (that is, in my flesh,) dwelleth no good thing: for to will is present with me; but how to perform that which is good I find not. For the good that I would I***

do not: but the evil which I would not, that I do. Now if I do that I would not, it is no more I that do it, but sin that dwelleth in me. I find then a law, that when I would do good, evil is present with me. For I delight in the law of God after the inward man." (Romans 18-22 KJV)

"This say then, Walk in the Spirit, and ye shall not fulfill the lust of the flesh. For the flesh lusteth against the Spirit, and the Spirit against the flesh: and these are contrary the one to the other: so that ye cannot do the things that ye would." (Galatians 5:16–17 KJV)

The Gift of the Holy Spirit

"But the Comforter, which is the Holy Ghost, whom the Father will send in my name, he shall teach you all things, and bring to your remembrance, whatsoever I have said unto you." (John 14:26 KJV)

"But when He, the Spirit of Truth (the Truth-giving Spirit) comes, He will guide you into all the Truth (the whole, full truth). For He will not speak His own message [on His own authority]; but he will tell whatever He hears [from the Father; He will give the message that has been given to Him], and He will announce and declare to you the things that

are to come [that will happen in the future]."
(John 16:13 AMP)

The Holy Spirit. The Revealer. God, in his mercy and grace, has given us an internal tour-guide, counselor and enabler as we journey on to fulfill His divine purpose for our lives. As we continue to seek God for our purpose and as we endeavor to accomplish the plan, the Holy Spirit equips us with the wisdom, knowledge and power to successfully accomplish all that God has assigned to us. The Holy Spirit is the Power of God.

> *"But ye shall receive power, after that the Holy Ghost is come unto you: and ye shall be witnesses unto me both in Jerusalem, and in all Judea, and in Samaria, and unto the uttermost part of the earth." (Acts 1:8 KJV)*

The Holy Spirit reveals the truth and gives us understanding of the truth that is revealed.

> *"But God hath revealed them unto us by his Spirit: for the Spirit searcheth all things, yea, the deep things of God." (I Corinthians 2:10 KJV)*

> *"He [The Holy Spirit] shall glorify me: for he shall receive of mine, and shall shew it unto you." (John 16:4 KJV)*

> *"And it was revealed unto him by the Holy Ghost, that he should not see death, before he had seen the Lord's Christ." (Luke 2:26 KJV)*

God Wants to Reveal His Plan To You

God desires to give you the revelation of wisdom and a degree of knowledge as to who He is. He does this so that you may know your calling (the purpose and plan for your life).

> ***"The eyes of your understanding being enlightened; that ye may know what is the hope of his calling, and what the riches of the glory of his inheritance in the saints." (Ephesians 1:8 KJV)***

He wants you to know your purpose. He wishes to inform you of the riches that He has already invested in you. He wants you to know what He has already given you, not what He is going to give, but what He has already given you. However, You need the Spirit of revelation to come upon you so that your understanding will be opened; so that you will be receptive to all that is being uncovered.

> ***"That the God of our Lord Jesus Christ, the Father of glory, may give unto you the spirit of wisdom and revelation in the knowledge of him." (Ephesians 1:17 KJV)***

> ***"And the spirit of the LORD shall rest upon him, the spirit of wisdom and understanding, the spirit of counsel and might, the spirit of knowledge and of the fear of the LORD." (Isaiah 11:2 KJV)***

God wants you to understand that He has a hope (optimism, expectation) for you. He wants you to know that, when He created you, He had a hope, a wish, and a purpose for you. This hope that God has is that His purpose for you be

Knowing Your Purpose

fulfilled in the earth. To ensure your ability to achieve the awesome tasks that He has assigned, God has given you a precious commodity, which is the Holy Spirit, to enable, guide and sustain you until you have completed all that God has planned for you. Prayerfully allow the scriptures to minister to you.

> *"For I know the thoughts that I think toward you, saith the LORD, thoughts of peace, and not of evil, to give you an expected end." (Jeremiah 29:11 KJV)*

Chapter Four Reflections

1. How can you be assured of the fact that no strategy can prevail against you?

2. Name some Old Testament characters that God revealed His plan to.

3. Name some New Testament characters that God revealed His plan to.

4. Which of these characters do you admire most? Why?

5. Why is patience needed in seeking God for your purpose?

6. Give five reasons, according to scripture, that reveal Jesus' purpose.

7. What are the three baptisms? Which of the three have you experienced? Explain.

8. Find the Old Testament scripture that confirms Luke 4:18-19.

9. Why should you submit to the Holy Spirit?

10. List some scriptures that the Apostle Paul wrote concerning the subduing of his flesh.

11. In compliance with this book, what are some of the names of the Holy Spirit?

12. What are some of the functions of the Holy Spirit?

13. How does the Holy Spirit help you seek out and explore the riches that God has already deposited within you?

14. What is God's hope for you, according to Chapter Four?

Chapter 5

✦ ✦ ✦

You Must Seek God For His Plan Concerning You

Although God desires whole-heartedly to reveal Himself to us, He has prerequisites for the distribution of this divine revelation. God has made available to man every avenue to this road of revelation. He has given us direct access to Him, through his Son, Christ Jesus. He has imparted into us grace, the ability to obtain knowledge and understanding via the Gift of the Holy Spirit. Yet, in His equity, He has also given us a will and we must choose to receive this revelation by means of diligent, persistent, and consistent seeking of it.

> *"I love them that love me; And those that seek me diligently shall find me." (Proverbs 8:17 KJV)*

"And ye shall seek me, and find me, when ye shall search for me with all your heart." (Jeremiah 29:13 KJV)

"Making known unto us the mystery of his will, according to his good pleasure which he purposed in him." (Ephesians 1:9 KJV)

"And to make all men see what is the dispensation of the mystery which for ages hath been hid in God who created all things." (Ephesians 3:9 KJV)

"That their hearts may be comforted, they being knit together in love, and unto all riches of the full assurance of understanding, that they may know the mystery of God, [even] Christ." (Colossians 2:2 KJV)

God has surely availed himself, likewise, we must give ourselves over to receiving all that is available.

Relationship Building

Relationship. The word in itself makes a statement. It refers to an association, a connection, an affiliation, a rapport, a bond or a link to God. In order to receive divine revelation from God, we must indeed have a relationship with Him. In endeavoring to seek the divine purpose and plan for our lives, we must work diligently at developing a close and very personal relationship with God. We must learn how to sincerely offer praise and worship to God. We need to increase the magnitude of our prayer life. It is imperative to study the Word of God, obtaining knowledge and building ourselves up in truth. We must also follow the example and submit to the government of our God-given leadership (our pastors), so that we may mature in the things of God. These key elements of relationship building are essential in the continued revelation of God's plan for our lives.

Sincere praise has been proven throughout the Word of God to be effective in building a relationship with God, causing us to come closer to or make a connection with God.

> *"It came to pass, when the trumpeters and singers were as one, to make one sound to be heard in praising and thanking Jehovah; and when they lifted up their voice with the trumpets and cymbals and instruments of music, and praised Jehovah, [saying], For he is good; for his loving kindness [endureth] for ever; that then the house was filled with a cloud, even the house of Jehovah, so that the priests could not stand to minister by reason of the cloud: for the glory of Jehovah filled the house of God." (II Chronicles 5:13-14 KJV)*

Pure worship gets God's attention and opens the door of opportunity for you to make your petition known unto him. It also compels Him to answer.

It has always been God's desire for His creation to worship Him. From the very beginning God created man to fellowship (koinonia), to come into His presence, to sup with Him.

> *"And they heard the voice of the LORD God walking in the garden in the cool of the day: and Adam and his wife hid themselves from the presence of the LORD God amongst the trees of the garden." (Genesis 3:8 KJV)*

After Adam, the male, and Adam, the female, disobeyed, God still sought for man to worship Him. The tabernacle that Moses was instructed to erect was simply God's temporary solution for man to approach Him for worship. Each compartment, from the outer court to the Holy of Holies was God extending to man a way of approach, speaking of Jesus Christ being the ultimate way.

> *"God is a Spirit: and they that worship Him must worship Him in spirit and in truth." (John 4:24 KJV)*

> *"And behold, there came to him a leper and worshipped him, saying, Lord, if thou wilt, thou canst make me clean. And he stretched forth his hand, and touched him, saying, I will; be thou made clean. And straightway his leprosy was cleansed." (Matthew 8:2-3 KJV)*

Frequent study of the Word of God shapes our understanding so that we are able to receive the revelation that God gives us as the divine truth.

> *"It is the glory of God to conceal a thing: but the honour of kings is to search out a matter." (Proverbs 25:2 KJV)*

> *"Search the scriptures; for in them ye think ye have eternal life: and they are they which testify of me." (John 5:39 KJV)*

For in the scriptures lie all of the answers that we seek; we only need them to be illuminated by the Holy Spirit so that they can be made applicable to our lives.

> *"For whatsoever things were written aforetime were written for our learning, that we through patience and comfort of the scriptures might have hope." (Romans 15:4 KJV)*

Another important aspect of building a relationship with God is submission to the leadership that He has placed us under. This consists of our Pastor and the other five-fold ministry gifts that God gave to the Body of Christ.

> *"And he gave some, apostles; and some, prophets; and some, evangelists; and some, pastors and teachers; For the perfecting of the saints, for the work of the ministry, for the edifying of the body of Christ: Till we all come in the unity of the faith, and of the knowledge of the Son of God, unto a perfect man, unto the measure of the stature of the fullness of Christ." (Ephesians 4: 11-13 KJV)*

Our response to the government of our God-given leadership is crucial to our advancement in relationship building efforts with God. God has placed a heightened degree of wisdom, knowledge, understanding, insight, anointing and discipline in our leaders that is tailored specifically for our spiritual growth. Irreverence, disobedience or indifference to them and the instructions that they give to us, can cause us to stifle our spiritual growth and hinder our relationship with God.

It is essential that you believe the man or woman of God that has watch for your soul is truly that...of God. Many people of God abort, hinder or prolong their time of development because they may feel that their overseer is delaying their purpose. Not true. An overseer will not attempt to hinder or prolong what God has given you to do. However, that overseer must be certain that you are prepared and mature enough to be released. Many lives can and will be affected positively as well as negatively.

> *"And I will set up shepherds over them which shall feed them: and they shall fear no more, nor be dismayed, neither shall they be lacking, saith the LORD." (Jeremiah 23:4 KJV)*

> *"Believe in the LORD your God, so shall ye be established; believe his prophets, so shall ye prosper." (II Chronicles 20:20 KJV)*

These components of relationship building are vital in seeking your God-given purpose. As with most things in life, you will only become more fluent or confident in these areas by means of sincere application and consistent use. The time that you invest communing with God by means of praise, worship, prayer, fasting, reading/studying the Word of God and following the example and tutelage of your God-given leadership directly reflects upon the strength or depth of your relationship with Him.

> *"For unto whomsoever much is given, of him shall much be required." (Luke 12:48 KJV)*

Faithfulness

Throughout the Word of God we see that faithfulness to the things of God, and even the things of man, not only caused the plan of God to be revealed but solidified. As a matter of fact, the majority of those in the Word of God that were rewarded as a result of their faithfulness were faithful first to the worldly things that were entrusted into their care.

Joseph, while he was yet in prison, was given authority even over the other prisoners as a result of His faithfulness.

> *"And the keeper of the prison committed to Joseph's hand all the prisoners that were in the prison; and whatsoever they did there, he was the doer of it. The keeper of the prison looked not to any thing that was under his hand; because the LORD was with him, and that which he did, the LORD made it to prosper." (Genesis 39: 22-23 KJV)*

David's faithfulness with the care of his father's sheep caused him to be appointed king over a nation.

> *"And David said unto Saul, Thy servant kept his father's sheep, and there came a lion and a bear, and took the lamb out of the flock: And I went out after him, and smote him, and delivered it out of his mouth: and when*

> *he arose against me, I caught him by his beard, and smote him, and slew him." (I Samuel 17: 34-35 KJV)*

Hananiah's displayed faithfulness and fear (reverence) of God caused him to be placed as a ruler over Jerusalem.

> *"That I gave my brother Hanani, and Hananiah the ruler of the palace, charge over Jerusalem: for he was a faithful man, and feared God above many." (Nehemiah 7:2 KJV).*

Timothy's faithfulness unto his service of the Apostle Paul, caused him to be appointed pastor over a church.

> *"For this cause have I sent unto you Timotheus [Timothy], who is my beloved son, and faithful in the Lord, who shall bring you into remembrance of my ways which be in Christ, as I teach every where in every church." (I Corinthians 4:17 KJV)*

Faithfulness is not just confined to diligence of activity; it also encompasses trust. God must be able to trust and entrust you with His plan. God is all knowing. He knows that we are as babes at the beginning of our walk with Him. Thus, He does not give us more than we are able to handle. In fact, at times God will allow us to enter into situations or be presented with circumstances that will test (try) our faithfulness, our ability to be trusted.

> *"Moreover they reckoned not with the men, into whose hand they delivered the money*

> *to be bestowed on workmen: for they dealt faithfully." (II Kings 12:15 KJV)*
>
> *"And I made treasurers over the treasuries, Shelemiah the priest, and Zadok the scribe, and of the Levites, Pedaiah: and next to them was Hanan the son of Zaccur, the son of Mattaniah: for they were counted faithful, and their office was to distribute unto their brethren." (Nehemiah 13:13 KJV)*
>
> *"And in those days, when the number of the disciples was multiplied, there arose a murmuring of the Grecians against the Hebrews, because their widows were neglected in the daily ministration. Then the twelve called the multitude of the disciples unto them, and said, It is not reason that we should leave the word of God, and serve tables. Wherefore, brethren, look ye out among you seven men of honest report, full of the Holy Ghost and wisdom, whom we may appoint over this business." (Acts 6:1-3 KJV)*

In all of these instances, the appointed individuals were placed in a position of authority where they could have dealt deceitfully to gain substance for themselves, yet they remained trustworthy; they remained faithful. As a result, a heavy burden was lifted from the person(s) who appointed them to the duty, and some were later elevated to other areas of service.

We should follow the examples of faithfulness as illustrated in the lives of the men and women of God that He has made available to us. We should endeavor to give ourselves to frequent study of the 'great' men and women of the Bible and their beginnings. We will see that their meager beginning, coupled with faithfulness, was a major contributor to their godly success.

Just as faithfulness is pleasing to God, unfaithfulness is displeasing. God desires us to be faithful to other men and their vision. In doing so, you are learning and being trained to receive your own. This is your time to learn by being obedient to and working closely with your leader; to observe their steps of faith and their obedience toward God. Joshua learned from Moses, Elisha from Elijah, Timothy from Paul, Apollos from Priscilla and Aquila; the list goes on. Who is your Paul or even your Saul? David learned how to reign as king by serving Saul. He learned the correct way and some incorrect ways. We are to observe both, and follow only after that which is good.

> *"And if ye have not been faithful in that which is another man's, who shall give you that which is your own?" (Luke 16:12 KJV)*

Ask and Wait on God to Answer

As multifaceted as God is, He has made many things relatively simple for His elect. It is almost mind-boggling that the best way to discover the purpose and plan that God has for your life is to ASK Him!

> *"Ask, and it shall be given you; seek, and ye shall find; knock, and it shall be opened unto you." (Matthew 7:7 KJV)*

> *"If ye abide in me, and my words abide in you, ye shall ask what ye will, and it shall be done unto you." (John 15:7 KJV)*

> *"If any of you lack wisdom, let him ask of God, that giveth to all men liberally, and upbraideth not; and it shall be given him. But let him ask in faith, nothing wavering." (James 1:5-6 KJV)*

> *"And this is the confidence that we have in him, that, if we ask any thing according to his will, he heareth us: And if we know that he hear us, whatsoever we ask, we know that we have the petitions that we desired of him." (I John 5:14-15 KJV)*

After you have established a relationship with God; after you have exhibited and been deemed faithful unto the things of God; after you have developed confidence in God's ability to be God; all that you need to do is ask. Relationship building, faithfulness and faith in God place you in a position to inquire of God and receive a response. However, we must understand that God is not on our timetable; we are on His. As such, we must be patient and allow God to answer, and make a steadfast determination not to move until He does.

> *"But, beloved, be not ignorant of this one thing, that one day is with the Lord as a thousand years, and a thousand years as one day." (II Peter 3:8 KJV)*

We must be patient, trusting and preferring God's timing and will above our own.

> *"But if we hope for that we see not, then do we with patience wait for it." (Romans 8:25 KJV)*

> *"For ye have need of patience, that, after ye have done the will of God, ye might receive the promise." (Hebrews 10:36 KJV)*

We should also be mindful that patience, rather than presumptuous action, keeps us on course to fulfilling the purpose for our lives, even though it may not be clearly revealed.

> *"But let patience have her perfect work, that ye may be perfect and entire, wanting nothing." (James 1:4 KJV)*

> *"To everything there is a season, and a time to every purpose under heaven." (Ecclesiastes 3:1 KJV)*

In our asking and in our patient waiting for God to reveal His plan for our lives, it is important that we understand the principles of God. We should understand that God's moves are decent and orderly. He is not the author of nor a contributor to confusion. We should understand that although God moves differently depending on the situation or circumstance, His way or character is unchanging. He is still the same God today that He was yesterday and that He will be in the future. Finally, believing that God does not, cannot and will not lie; we can trust that He does nothing in the earth

You Must Seek God For His Plan Concerning You

without first revealing it via His prophets (His mouthpieces in the earth), for he decreed it in His Word.

> *"Surely the Lord God will do nothing, but he revealeth his secret unto his servants the prophets." (Amos 3:7 KJV)*
>
> *"Jesus Christ the same yesterday, and to-day, and forever." (Hebrew 13:8 KJV)*
>
> *"For God is not the author of confusion, but of peace, as in all churches of the saints." (I Corinthians 14:33 KJV)*
>
> *"God is not a man, that he should lie; neither the son of man, that he should repent: hath he said, and shall he not do it? or hath he spoken, and shall he not make it good?" (Numbers 23:19 KJV)*
>
> *"The thing that hath been, it is that which shall be; and that which is done is that which shall be done: and there is no new thing under the sun." (Ecclesiastes 1:9 KJV)*

Chapter Five Reflections

1. What must you do to receive revelation from God?

2. How can you develop a relationship with God?

3. List Old Testament means of fellowship with God.

4. How can we fellowship in this dispensation (here and now)?

5. Why is worship so important?

6. What type of relationship do you have with your leaders?

7. Can this affect your relationship with God? Explain how.

8. Define faithfulness.

9. What Biblical patriarchs exhibited faithfulness and were promoted in the kingdom of God?

10. How is unfaithfulness rewarded?

11. How does a good relationship with God build confidence in you?

Chapter 6

✦✦✦

Once The Purpose and Plan Are Revealed

After you have sought God and received the purpose and plan that He has for your life, you must begin to walk therein. The focal activity in that statement is WALK. Walk, according to the *New Heritage Dictionary*, simply means to be in constant motion. You must be in constant pursuit of God's will concerning your life. You should not be so excited about receiving your purpose that you forget about His plan and His timing. You should always remember that God gives the increase. He has promised to establish you. He has decreed that He would make your name great.

> *"But they that wait upon the LORD shall renew their strength; they shall mount up with wings as eagles; they shall run, and not*

> *be weary; and they shall walk, and not faint."*
> *(Isaiah 40:31 KJV)*

> *"But let patience have her perfect work, that ye may be perfect and entire, wanting nothing." (James 1:4 KJV)*

> *"Commit thy way unto the LORD; trust also in him; and he shall bring it to pass." (Psalms 37:5 KJV)*

> *"...Yea, I have spoken it, I will also bring it to pass; I have purposed it, I will also do it." (Isaiah 46:11b KJV)*

In looking at the example of Christ Jesus, though He was God manifested in flesh, He did not draw any unnecessary attention to himself. As a matter of fact, He made of himself no reputation; nonetheless, He made a phenomenal impact upon the people that He encountered during His journey here on earth. The result of His humility and effectiveness in completing the plan and purpose for which He was manifested, caused God the Father to highly exalt Him, to make the name of Jesus higher than any other name.

> *"Let this mind be in you, which was also in Christ Jesus: Who, being in the form of God, thought it not robbery to be equal with God: But made himself of no reputation, and took upon him the form of a servant, and was made in the likeness of men." (Philippians 2:5-7 KJV)*

> *"I have glorified thee on the earth: I have finished the work which thou gavest me to do. And now, O Father, glorify thou me with thine own self with the glory which I had with thee before the world was." (John 17:4-5 KJV)*

Similarly, we should aim to move forward in humility, not desiring to make a name for ourselves, but desiring wholeheartedly to be effective in accomplishing the will of God. We must not confuse humility with timidity, because God does want us to make an impact. He desires that we shake things up a bit. He wants us to positively influence someone. He wants us to be instrumental in turning someone's life around. He wants us to positively affect others. He desires that we be infectious with the good news of Christ Jesus. He wants us to win back souls to the Kingdom of God. Thus, timidity cannot be a factor. We must assume the position of authority that was given to us by our Lord Jesus Christ.

> *"And all things are of God, who hath reconciled us to himself by Jesus Christ, and hath given to us the ministry of reconciliation." (II Corinthians 5:18 KJV)*

> *"For the Son of man is as a man taking a far journey, who left his house, and gave authority to his servants, and to every man his work, and commanded the porter to watch." (Mark 13:34 KJV)*

Even in assuming this position of inherited authority, we must remember that God gives the increase. It is God's plan. He orchestrates the plan and we are to follow his directive. As with a natural orchestra, all of the musicians have the sheet music for the selections to be played, however, the magnificence of the selection is only portrayed when all of the musicians play precisely as directed by the conductor. Should one cord be played improperly or inopportunely, the most majestic musical selection can become merely noise made by musical instruments.

Similarly, God equips us with the plan to complete our purpose. Though we are equipped with the plan, we must continue to follow His leading. Otherwise, we risk turning the glory of God's completed masterpiece into the gloom of our fleshly ways.

Don't Force It

In seeking the purpose and plan that God has for your life, it is equally essential that you seek the timing for the manifestation of the plan. All too frequently the people of God, though well intentioned, abort or temporarily stunt the development of the plan of God in their lives due to impatience, insensitivity and/or ignorance. The present day church is not the only culprit of these acts. The Word of God illustrates many examples of those who acted prematurely (Abraham & Sarah); insensitively (Moses) and ignorantly (David). We must endeavor to perform the plan of God according to His specifications and timing. If we do this, God has promised to give the increase. Yet, if we venture out in our own strength and ability in attempts to hasten the total manifestation of God's purpose in our lives, the responsibility of increase remains with us.

Once the Purpose and Plan Are Revealed

> *"So then neither is he that planteth any thing, neither he that watereth; but God that giveth the increase." (I Corinthians 3:7 KJV)*

> *"To every thing there is a season, and a time to every purpose under the heaven." (Ecclesiastes 3:1 KJV)*

We must understand that God is a strategist. In fact, He is THE Strategist. From Genesis through Revelation, God has baffled mankind with His methods of fulfilling His purpose. In Genesis, Satan attempted to stifle the plan of God for man by facilitating in man's rebellion against God. However, God had already instituted the plan of Jesus Christ before the world was formed.

> *"Yea, hath God said, Ye shall not eat of every tree of the garden? And the woman said unto the serpent, We may eat of the fruit of the trees of the garden: But of the fruit of the tree which is in the midst of the garden, God hath said, Ye shall not eat of it, neither shall ye touch it, lest ye die. And the serpent said unto the woman, Ye shall not surely die: For God doth know that in the day ye eat thereof, then your eyes shall be opened, and ye shall be as gods, knowing good and evil. And when the woman saw that the tree was good for food, and that it was pleasant to the eyes, and a tree to be desired to make one wise, she took of the fruit thereof, and did eat, and gave also unto her husband with her; and he did eat." (Genesis 3: 1-6 KJV)*

> *"And all that dwell upon the earth shall worship him, whose names are not written in the book of life of the Lamb slain from the foundation of the world." (Revelation 13:8 KJV)*

Though Moses knew that he was sent to bring God's elect out of Egypt, he probably never expected to destroy Pharaoh and his army as well as spoil the wealth of the Egyptians by simply stretching forth his rod over the Red Sea.

> *"But lift thou up thy rod, and stretch out thine hand over the sea, and divide it: and the children of Israel shall go on dry ground through the midst of the sea. And I, behold, I will harden the hearts of the Egyptians, and they shall follow them: and I will get me honour upon Pharaoh, and upon all his host, upon his chariots, and upon his horsemen." Exodus (13:16-17)*

In I Samuel, God appointed David king while Saul was still on the throne. Little did David know that his preparation for kingship would come from fleeing Saul, hiding in caves and fighting many life-threatening battles with little or no resources.

> *"David therefore departed thence, and escaped to the cave Adullam: and when his brethren and all his father's house heard it, they went down thither to him. And every one that was in distress, and every one that was in debt, and every one that was discon-*

> tented, gathered themselves unto him; and he became a captain over them: and there were with him about four hundred men. And David went thence to Mizpeh of Moab: and he said unto the king of Moab, Let my father and my mother, I pray thee, come forth, and be with you, till I know what God will do for me." (1 Samuel 22:1-3)

Judas did not understand that by betraying Jesus, he was fulfilling prophecy and solidifying the salvation of all who would believe in Christ and receive Him as Lord.

> "Judas then, having received a band of men and officers from the chief priests and Pharisees, cometh thither with lanterns and torches and weapons. Jesus therefore, knowing all things that should come upon him, went forth, and said unto them, Whom seek ye?" (John 18:3-4 KJV)

Who would have ever thought that Saul, an avid persecutor of the Church; would later become Paul, a pioneer of the Gospel?

> "And I said, Lord, they know that I imprisoned and beat in every synagogue them that believed on thee: And when the blood of thy martyr Stephen was shed, I also was standing by, and consenting unto his death, and kept the raiment of them that slew him. And he said unto me, Depart: for I will send thee far hence unto the Gentiles." (Acts 22:19-21 KJV)

Understanding that the God that we serve is a strategist, should give us great confidence in Him and our waiting for His direction to carry out His ultimate plan.

Allow God to Bring His Plan to Fruition

Once we know our purpose and understand that God has a strategy for the accomplishing of the plan that He has for our lives; we must allow God to bring it pass. We must remember that we are merely vessels in the eyes of God. We are simply instruments or tools that God uses to complete the building of His earthen edifice. Vessels don't fill themselves...they are filled. Tools don't use themselves...they are used. As such, we must earnestly desire to be quality vessels prepared for God's use.

> *"But in a great house there are not only vessels of gold and of silver, but also of wood and of earth; and some to honour, and some to dishonour. If a man therefore purge himself from these, he shall be a vessel unto honour, sanctified, and meet for the master's use, and prepared unto every good work."*
> *(II Timothy 2:20-21 KJV)*

This belief invokes a true spirit of humility when handling the plan of God. As God begins to manifest His plan through us and is glorified, we must remain grounded. The realization that the extent of our contribution to the fulfilling of God's plan is simply our obedience and availability (being willing and ready) assists greatly in keeping us grounded as God takes us to higher heights and deeper depths.

> *"For whosoever exalteth himself shall be abased; and he that humbleth himself shall be exalted."* (Luke 14:11 KJV)
>
> *"Humble yourselves in the sight of the Lord, and he shall lift you up."* (James 4:10 KJV)
>
> *"By humility and the fear of the LORD are riches, and honour, and life."* (Proverbs 22:4)

The humility as described does not render to low self-esteem or low self-worth. Actually, this humility leads to a soberness, maturity, and confidence that can only be attained by experiencing one's inability being replaced by God's unlimited ability to accomplish His plan.

> *"But he giveth more grace [ability]. Wherefore he saith, God resisteth the proud, but giveth grace [ability] unto the humble."* (James 4:6 KJV)

In order to be truly effective in accomplishing the total plan that God has for our lives, we must realize our natural limits and boundaries. Likewise, it is equally as important to realize the ability of God and His Spirit that He has caused to dwell within us. This is where the glory of God is manifested, when (as with Abraham, Moses, Joshua, David, Jesus Christ, Paul and John) we understand where our ability ends and the supernatural ability of the Spirit of God begins.

Chapter Six Reflections

1. Name some pitfalls of attempting to gain a reputation.

2. Define humility.

3. Define timidity.

4. Name some ways that you can find out about the plan of God for your life.

5. How can you become a vessel of Glory?

6. How can low self-esteem affect God's plan for you?

Chapter 7

✦ ✦ ✦

Knowing Your Purpose

God reveals himself to His people for a reason, for a plan and for a purpose. If you have not received God's plan for your life, you can begin by simply inquiring of Him. Purpose to set time apart and ask the Lord, "Why have you revealed Yourself to me? Why have you saved me? What do you want me to do now?" He will begin to reveal Himself to you. Your purpose will be revealed to you in seeking God through prayer, through the taught Word, through the written Word, through anointed vessels that God has ordained to teach you the truth through praise and worship, through just lying in the presence of God. In the sincerity and consistent application of these, God will not withhold His plan from you. Then, once the plan for your life has been revealed, walk confidently therein.

Walking in God's Plan for Your Life

Once God reveals and you receive the plan for your life, you must become fully persuaded of that revelation and have the utmost confidence in God's ability to bring it to total manifestation. You should hide that revelation in your heart and allow God to confirm and manifest it in His timing. Be bold and tenacious in carrying out the plan of God. Don't allow people to counsel or persuade you to operate outside of the plan and timing that God has for you. Carry out all divinely assigned tasks expecting success. Do not seek the approval of people or attempt to flow in the mainstream. Resolve in your heart that the only validation and approval that is necessary in accomplishing the plan of God is from God Himself, knowing that as long as you are walking obediently and sincerely according to His will, He is well pleased.

Continue to Seek God for Guidance

Daily communion with God will aid in the effectiveness of your completing His total plan for your life. It is important to understand that although the plan of God for your life does not change, the methods may change, or God may reveal more of His plan to you. Neglecting to have daily fellowship with God or yielding your members to clearly hear from God may cause you to hinder, stunt or abort a mission that God has for your life.

You should not become common with your handling of the things of God. You should not assume that because God has revealed a portion of His plan to you, you know all that you need to know. God may have more for you, and becoming arrogant with His initial revelation may cause you to miss the mark.

Knowing Your Purpose

Endeavor to keep your spiritual ear fastened to the mouth of God. Seek the plan of God for your life each day. Become acclimated to hearing from God on minor issues, such as what apparel you should wear each day, and being obedient to his instruction. Sensitize your spirit man to responding to the leading of the Holy Spirit by asking which route He would like you to take home from work, and then following His direction. Seeking and adhering to God's direction in minor matters will no doubt aid in your hearing and following his daily guidance in spiritual matters.

I remember, when I was a babe in Christ, how the Holy Spirit began to speak to me in everyday situations. As I was preparing to leave home for church, the Holy Spirit reminded me to check the side door, making certain that it was locked. Being a babe, I shrugged it away saying within myself, "Oh, I know the door is secure; it's okay." However, upon my return, I found the door UNLOCKED! But thanks be to God, nothing had been disturbed. That is just one of many incidents that God has used to make me sensitive to His voice. We must always be sensitive to the leading and guidance of the Holy Spirit in all things.

> *"Trust in the LORD with all thine heart; and lean not to thine own understanding. In all thy ways acknowledge Him, and He shall direct thy paths." (Proverbs 3:5-6 KJV)*

> *"Howbeit when he, the Spirit of truth, is come, he will guide you into all truth: for he shall not speak of himself; but whatsoever he shall hear, that shall he speak: and he will shew you things to come." (John 16:13 KJV)*

Chapter Seven Reflections

1. Why does God reveal Himself to His people?

2. Why is it important to have confidence in God's revealed plan for your life?

3. Express how daily fellowship with God keeps you focused.

4. How can your routine activities be directed by God?

5. How will this enhance your overall relationship with God?

6. Name some ways that the Holy Spirit has given you day-to-day guidance.

Chapter 8

✦ ✦ ✦

God May Have More For You

More Than One Mission

Our Lord Jesus Christ is our perfect example in every circumstance and situation that we encounter in life. Though Jesus' purpose was to redeem man back unto the Father and to defeat the works of Satan, He had many missions as he journeyed on to complete His work.

The following is an outline of His missions:

I) Phase I
    a) Submitting obediently to His parents
    b) Patiently waiting for His time for ministry
    c) Seeking out and submitting to baptism via John the Baptist

II) Phase II
    a) Gathering the disciples

b) Training the disciples in the Word of God and illustrating to them the power of God via healings, deliverances and other miracles
c) Administering the Sacraments of Foot Washing and the Holy Communion

III) Phase III
   a) Dying for the sins of man
   b) Descending into Hell and defeating Satan
   c) Raising from the dead and preparing the disciples for ministry
   d) Ascending into heaven
   e) Giving gifts unto men

IV) Phase IV
   a) Taking His rightful place seated at the right hand of the Father
   b) Sending the Gift of the Holy Spirit
   c) Reigning as King and Lord of All
   d) Judging the World

In studying the life of Christ and becoming aware of the missions that led to the completion of his ultimate purpose, it is evident that obedience to God in phase one of His life led Him to the next phase and finally on to completing the total will of God for His life in the earth. As you journey on to complete the will that God has for your life, know that there may be many missions on the road to fulfilling the total purpose. Like Jesus Christ, your obedience to God will ensure that you successfully complete each mission and ultimately your purpose for existing.

God May Have More For You

Can God Trust You Enough To Assign More Than One Mission to You

Know for certain that God has a plan and purpose for your life. Know also that the success of your accomplishing that plan is entirely up to you. You must make a choice to be obedient to the Word of God. You must make a conscious effort to get and remain in the will of God. He has already placed inside of you everything necessary to accomplish the task. He has promised to give angels charge over you to undergird you, to bear you up, to make sure that His will is accomplished in the earth through you. When you begin to move according to the will of God, He will give you all the support that you need. He will send the help. He will ensure your success. Once you begin to walk in His will you become God's responsibility, and there is no failure in Him. Again, the choice is yours. God has given man a will. We must make a decision, coupled with corresponding effort, that our will shall align with the will of God.

God may have many missions for you, yet your obedience, faithfulness and willingness in completing the first mission will have a direct effect on God granting you stewardship over other missions. The first mission may be as simple as submitting to your God-given leadership, or as complex as starting a church. However minute or grand the initial phase of God's plan for your life may be, your reward will be in the handling of it. In looking throughout the Word of God, there are many instances where God has only revealed the next phase of a person's plan and purpose upon them successfully completing the first (Moses, Elisha, Jacob, Joseph, Apostle Paul). There were also instances where man has been considered ineligible to handle further the plan of God due to rebellion, fear and disobedience (Adam, Moses, Elijah).

Will you allow the total plan of God to be manifested in your life? Will you submit totally to the leading and guidance of God in carrying out His plan? Will you allow God to manifest success in you? Will you remain willing and obedient until you have finished the course for your life? Will you allow the glory of God to be seen in your life? The choice is yours. God has already completed His work in your life. It is up to you to build a solid relationship with God, to seek out the purpose of God for your life, to inquire of God daily of His plan for your life, to be obedient in performing the instruction of God, that He has already ordained, decreed and solidified your success. Will you receive it?

The Author's Heart

Now that you have completed this book, and hopefully answered the questions listed after each chapter, I pray that you now have a deeper understanding of how to know and achieve your purpose. We by no means claim to have all the answers to your many questions. We simply wish to encourage you to follow after God, seeking him, for He does have all the answers and solutions to your questions. Our prayer and desire for you is to have good success in all that you do, to the glory of God the Father.

Closing Prayer

Father in Jesus' name, I thank you for those that have invested their time to read, study and apply the principles written in this book. May you by your Spirit enlighten those that hunger and thirst after you. Your Word declares that they shall be filled and those that seek shall find. Thank you Father for bringing us to our expected end. Thank you Holy Spirit for your guidance in all that we do. Amen!

Hope Evangelical Ministries

Hope Evangelical Ministries ("Where Eagles Gather") is an international ministry located in the metropolitan area of Detroit, Michigan. Bishop Dr. Frankie H. Young, Apostle, is founder and Senior Pastor, Reverend Michael A. Davis, Sr. is Pastor and Reverend Kevin L. Young is Co-Pastor. "Hope" is a strong, Word-based ministry where emphasis is placed on the pure Word of God, prayer, praise and worship. The mission statement of "Hope" is to create an atmosphere of love as we minister to the total man: body, soul and spirit. We aspire to be a beacon of light in the city, nation and world; equipping men and women to effectively fulfill their call to ministry.

If you desire to order additional copies of this book, please fill out the order form and mail or fax it to:

Hope Evangelical Ministries
4600 Livernois
Detroit, Michigan 48210-2442
Telephone: 313-894-7232
Fax: 313-894-7115

We invite you to visit our website: www.hopeevanmin.org to obtain further information regarding Hope Evangelical Ministries, the pastors, our auxiliaries and ministries.

- -

Order Form

Each book is $12.95. Please include $3.00 for shipping.

Name: _____

Address: _____

City: _____ **State:** _____ **Zip:** _____

Telephone: _____

No. of Copies: _____ **Amount Enclosed:** _____